Creative Crafts for Kids

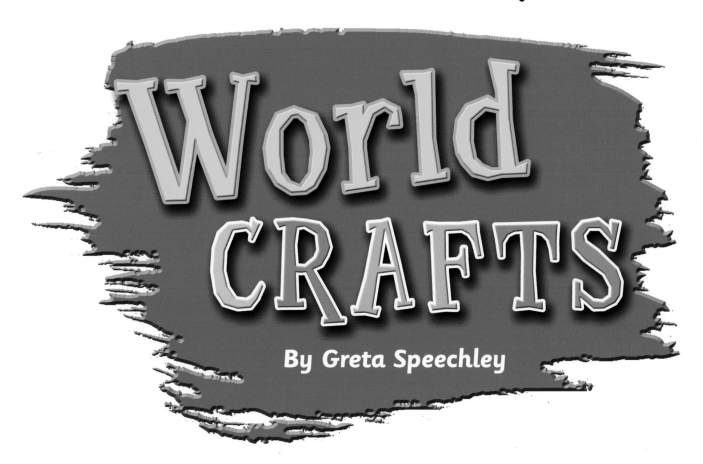

World CRAFTS

By Greta Speechley

Gareth Stevens
Publishing

Please visit our Web site www.garethstevens.com. For a free color catalog of all our high-quality books, call toll free 1-800-542-2595 or fax 1-877-542-2596.

Library of Congress Cataloging-in-Publication Data
Speechley, Greta, 1949-
    World crafts / Greta Speechley.
        p. cm. — (Creative crafts for kids)
    Includes index.
    ISBN 978-1-4339-3561-9 (library binding)
    ISBN 978-1-4339-3562-6 (pbk.)
    ISBN 978-1-4339-3563-3 (6-pack)
    1. Handicraft—Juvenile literature. I. Title.
TT157.S655 2010
745.5—dc22   2009041574

Published in 2010 by
Gareth Stevens Publishing
111 East 14th Street, Suite 349
New York, NY 10003

© 2010 The Brown Reference Group Ltd.

For Gareth Stevens Publishing:
Art Direction: Haley Harasymiw
Editorial Direction: Kerri O'Donnell

For The Brown Reference Group Ltd:
Editorial Director: Lindsey Lowe
Managing Editor: Tim Harris
Children's Publisher: Anne O'Daly
Design Manager: David Poole
Production Director: Alastair Gourlay

Picture Credits:
All photographs: Martin Norris
Front Cover: Shutterstock: Photosani and Martin Norris

Manufactured in the United States of America
1 2 3 4 5 6 7 8 9   12 11 10

CPSIA compliance information: Batch #BRW0102GS: For further information contact Gareth Stevens, New York, New York at 1-800-542-2595.

Contents

Introduction

The projects in this book are based on traditional designs from all over the world. Learn how to make a Native American dream catcher, an Australian didgeridoo, or a fantastic lion mask from Africa. Follow the photographs and easy instructions for your very own world tour!

YOU WILL NEED

Each project includes a list of all the things you need.

Before you buy new materials, have a look at home to see what you could use instead. For example, you can cut cardboard shapes out of empty cereal boxes or Christmas cards.

You can buy other items, such as air-drying clay, raffia, and crochet thread at department stores or craft shops.

Getting started

Read the steps for the project first.

Gather together all the items you need.

Cover your work surface with newspaper.

Wear an apron, or change into old clothes.

A message for adults

All the projects in *World Crafts* have been designed for children to make, but occasionally they will need you to help. Some of the projects do require the use of sharp utensils, such as scissors and needles. Please read through the instructions before your child starts work.

A message for adults

This is how to make the patterns on pages 30 and 31. Using a pencil, trace the pattern onto tracing paper. To cut a pattern out of cardboard, turn the tracing over, and lay it onto the cardboard. Rub firmly over the pattern with a pencil. The shape will appear on the cardboard. Cut out the shape. Some of the patterns in this book are half patterns. To find out how to make a whole pattern using them, read the instructions for the project.

Making stencils

To make the stencil on page 31, follow the instructions for making a pattern; but instead of cutting out the shape, push your scissor points into the middle of the design. (Ask an adult to help you.) Carefully cut around the inside of the pencil outline, leaving a "window" in the paper or cardboard. This is the stencil.

When you have finished

 Wash paintbrushes, and put everything away.

 Put pens, pencils, paints, and glue in an old box or ice-cream container.

 Keep scissors and any other sharp items in a safe place.

 Stick needles and pins into a pincushion or a piece of scrap cloth.

BE SAFE

Look out for the safety boxes. They will appear whenever you need to ask an adult for help.

Ask an adult to help you use sharp scissors.

Mardi Gras tambourine

Mardi Gras is a festival held every year on Fat Tuesday. There are processions in the streets, and people dance and play musical instruments. New Orleans has one of the most famous Mardi Gras festivals in the world.

YOU WILL NEED

2 paper plates	beads
felt-tip pens	hole punch
dried beans or macaroni	clear glue
ribbon	scissors

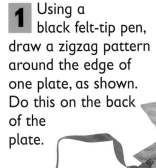

1 Using a black felt-tip pen, draw a zigzag pattern around the edge of one plate, as shown. Do this on the back of the plate.

2 Hold both plates together, face to face. Carefully cut a zigzag edge on both of the plates.

3 Draw a pattern on the back of each plate, and color it in with felt-tip pens. Copy the designs shown here, or draw your own patterns.

4 With the blank side of the plates facing you, put a handful of beans or macaroni in the middle of one plate. Put glue around the zigzag edge, and stick the plates together, trapping the beans or macaroni inside.

5 Using a hole punch, make holes in some of the zigzag points. Tie ribbons through the holes. To finish, thread beads onto the ribbons. Then shake!

Celtic window

This beautiful window is inspired by the circular pattern used for many Celtic stained-glass windows. Hang your window so that the sunlight shines through the colored cellophane.

YOU WILL NEED

thin black cardboard

tracing paper

pencil

scissors

white pencil

colored cellophane

double-sided tape

cotton thread

Ask an adult to help you use sharp scissors.

1 Trace the frame pattern on page 31. (See Making patterns, on page 5.) Lay the half pattern face down onto black cardboard. Rub over the outline with a pencil. The shape will appear on the cardboard. Flip the tracing over, line up the pattern, and trace back over the pencil lines to make the other half of the pattern. Cut out the frame. Push scissor points into the window to cut out the shapes. Ask an adult to help you.

2 Lay the frame onto black cardboard, and draw around the shape with a white pencil. Cut out a second frame.

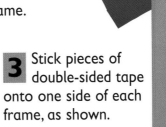

3 Stick pieces of double-sided tape onto one side of each frame, as shown.

4 Cut four quarter-circles of cellophane. Peel the backing off the double-sided tape on one frame, and stick the cellophane quarter-circles in position.

5 Peel the backing off the tape on the second frame. Carefully stick the two frames together. To finish, make a hole at the top of the window. Thread cotton through the hole to make a loop for hanging up your window.

Lion mask

The idea for this fabulous lion mask comes from West Africa. Animal masks were worn during ceremonial dances and were originally made from straw and grasses woven together.

YOU WILL NEED

thin yellow cardboard	2 pipe cleaners
red raffia	scissors
frilly red crêpe paper streamer	black felt-tip pen
thin elastic	clear glue
	large needle

1 To make the lion's face, draw a circle 9in (23cm) in diameter onto thin yellow cardboard. (An easy way to do this is to draw around a dinner plate.) Cut out the shape. Draw on features with a black felt-tip pen. Cut out the eyes.

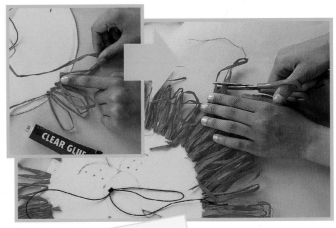

2 Thread a large needle with thin elastic, and make a hole at each side of the face. Ask an adult to help you do this. Pull the elastic through the holes, and adjust the length so that the mask fits around your head. Knot the ends of the elastic over the holes.

Ask an adult to help you use a sharp needle.

3 With the back of the mask facing you, glue lengths of raffia around the edge of the circle to make the mane. Trim off any straggly ends.

4 Fold the red crêpe paper streamer in half. Glue several rows of it close together to the front of the mask.

5 For the whiskers, make two holes at each side of the lion's mouth using a large needle. Ask an adult to help you. Fold the pipe cleaners in half, and poke them through the holes, as shown.

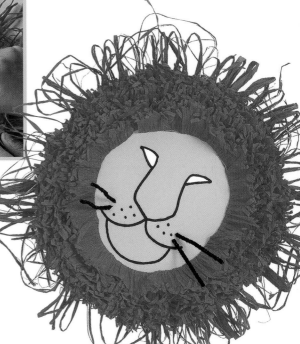

11

Indian mirror

Make this stunning mirror to hang on your bedroom wall. The frame is made from cardboard stuck onto a mirror tile and decorated with glitter, stickers, and a gold elephant.

YOU WILL NEED

mirror tile, 5¾in x 5¾in (15cm x 15cm)	paintbrush
	double-sided tape
pink cardboard	glitter glue
gold paper	glitter
shiny stickers	scissors
PVA glue	pencil
	tracing paper

1 Trace the patterns on page 30. (See Making patterns, on page 5.) Lay the half pattern for the frame face down onto pink cardboard. Rub over the outline with a pencil. The shape will appear on the cardboard. Flip the tracing over, line up the pattern, and trace back over the pencil lines to make the other half of the frame. Cut out the shape. Cut an elephant out of gold paper.

2 Stick long strips of double-sided tape to the back of the window frame, as shown.

3 Dilute a little PVA glue with water to make it easier to apply. Now paint PVA over the front of the window frame, leaving a narrow border around the edge.

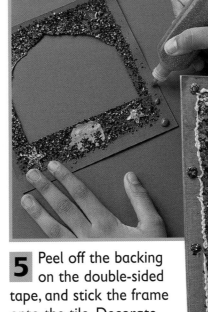

4 Stick the elephant to the frame. Sprinkle glitter all over the frame while the glue is still wet. Shake off excess glitter.

5 Peel off the backing on the double-sided tape, and stick the frame onto the tile. Decorate the frame with glitter glue and stickers. You can also glue a loop of string to the back so you can hang up the mirror.

13

Gambian bracelets

Try making these pretty woven bracelets to give to your friends as presents. They are based on a design from The Gambia in West Africa.

CLEAR GLUE

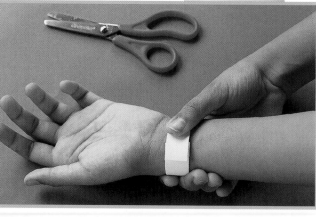

1 Cut a strip from a plastic bottle about ¾in (2cm) wide and long enough to fit around your wrist, including an extra 1in (2.5cm). Ask an adult to help you do this.

2 Cut two lengths of each color crochet thread as long as the plastic strip plus an extra 2in (5cm). Stick one end of the colored threads and the black thread to one end of the plastic strip.

3 Wrap the black thread around the strip, covering the colored threads. Do this until you have covered about 1in (2.5cm) of the bracelet.

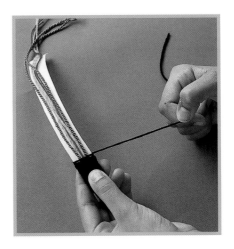

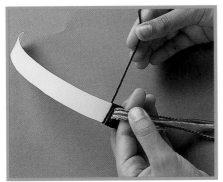

4 Lift up the colored threads. Now wrap the black thread around the plastic strip three times.

Ask an adult to help you cut the plastic bottle.

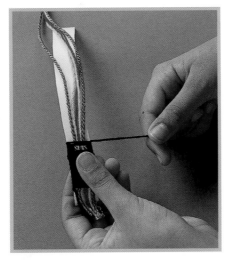

5 Lay the colored threads back down onto the plastic strip. Now wrap the black thread around the colored threads three times. Continue doing this until you are about 1in (2.5cm) from the end of the strip.

6 Dab glue onto the end of the bracelet, and stick the colored threads onto the plastic strip. Continue wrapping the black thread around the end of the bracelet, then glue in place. To finish, stick small pads of Velcro to both ends of the bracelet so you can fasten it around your wrist.

Dream catcher

Native American dream catchers are shaped like a circle to represent the whole universe. Hang it over your bed—good dreams are caught in the web, and bad ones escape through the holes.

YOU WILL NEED

metal ring (from a craft shop)	thick gold thread, 1yd (1m)
clear glue	beads
narrow ribbon, 1yd (1m)	feather
	large needle

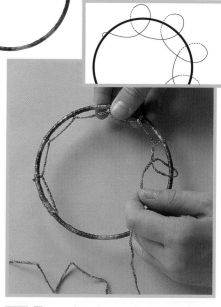

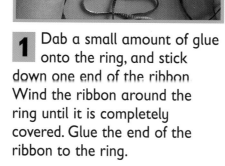

1 Dab a small amount of glue onto the ring, and stick down one end of the ribbon. Wind the ribbon around the ring until it is completely covered. Glue the end of the ribbon to the ring.

2 To make the web, loop the gold thread evenly around the ring, as shown in the diagram.

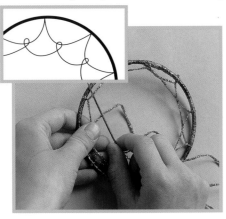

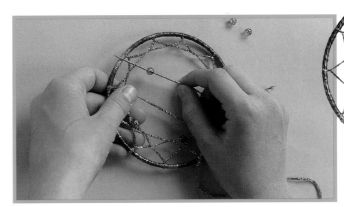

3 Continue making the web. Use the needle to push the thread through the loops, as shown, and pull the thread tight. Continue until you have made a second layer of loops.

4 Now thread a bead onto every other loop. Make one more layer of loops, and then tie the end of the thread neatly to the web.

Ask an adult to help you use a sharp needle.

5 Tie a large bead to a length of gold thread, and tie it to the middle of the dream catcher.

6 To make a tail, tie a feather onto a length of thread. Push beads onto the thread, and tie it to the bottom of the ring.

Didgeridoo

Didgeridoos are traditional wind instruments made by Native Australians. The shapes and patterns represent a bird's eye view of the country—just like a map. The wavy lines are snakes and roots, and the circles and lines represent animal burrows.

YOU WILL NEED

- long cardboard tube
- poster paints
- thick and thin paintbrushes
- cardboard (for palette)
- clear spray varnish

1 Mix together red, blue, yellow, and a little black paint to make a rich earthy brown. Using a thick paintbrush, paint on the first shape, as shown. This shape represents the burrows of a goanna (a type of lizard).

18

2 Paint a set of blue and orange wavy lines at both ends of the cardboard tube, as shown.

3 Paint different-sized shapes all over the rest of the tube, as shown, until the tube is completely covered.

4 Using the hard end of the paintbrush, add dots of color to the shapes. Use white dots to outline the main shapes.

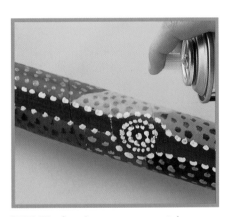

5 To finish, spray varnish over the tube. It will protect the tube and make the colors brighter. Ask an adult to help you do this.

HANDY HINT

Mixing colors

Native Australian painting is traditionally done in earthy colors. To deepen the color of the paints you use, add a little black paint. Here are some ways you can mix your own colors.

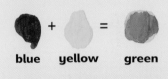

blue + yellow = green

yellow + red = orange

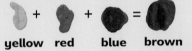

yellow + red + blue = brown

Ask an adult to help you use the spray varnish. Read the instructions on the packaging before you start.

19

Mexican armadillo

This cute little armadillo is made from air-drying clay, which is left to harden and then painted in bright colors. Follow the instructions on the packaging for drying and hardening the clay.

YOU WILL NEED

air-drying clay (from a craft shop)	paintbrush
	toothpicks
poster paints	sponge

1 To make the body, roll a ball of clay about the size of a tennis ball. Press your thumb into the middle, and hollow out the ball by squeezing the clay between your thumb and fingers. Work evenly all around the ball.

2 Turn the body shape over, and flatten the open edge by tapping it gently on a table. Now make a neck hole at the front of the body shape. Pull up the edges of the neck to make a raised collar, as shown.

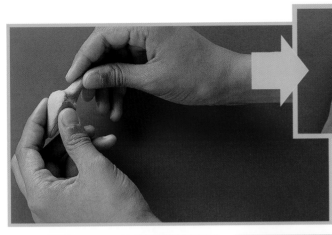

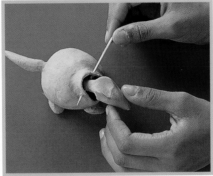

3 For the head, roll a small ball of clay. Form one end into a triangle shape and the other into a sausage shape. Pinch up the ears, as shown.

4 Roll four small balls of clay for the feet and a short sausage shape for the tail. Using a small piece of sponge, moisten the surfaces with water, and stick the feet and tail to the body. Blend the edges of the clay together.

5 Hold the head in the neck hole. Carefully push a toothpick through one side of the neck hole, into the neck, and out through the other side of the neck hole. Let the armadillo dry in a safe place.

6 When the clay has dried and hardened, remove the head from the body, and paint the armadillo in bright colors. To reattach the head, push the toothpick back through the holes in the neck and head, and trim off the ends with a pair of scissors. Ask an adult to help.

Ask an adult to help you trim the ends off the toothpick.

21

Chinese dragon

This colorful dragon would make a great decoration for Chinese New Year. You can attach the finished dragon to a garden stick to play with or hang it on a wall.

1 Trace the pattern on page 31. (See Making patterns, on page 5.) Lay the half pattern face down on red paper. Rub over the outline with a pencil. The shape will appear on the paper. Flip the tracing over, line up the pattern, and trace back over the pencil lines to make the other half of the dragon's head. Cut out the head shape. Go over the features with a black felt-tip pen. Fold the head at the dotted lines to make the center panel shown on the pattern.

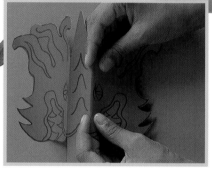

2 Color in the dragon's features using colored pencils and a gold pen.

22

3 To make the dragon's tail, cut a strip of red paper and a strip of gold paper the same width as the striking side of the matchbox and 36in (92cm) long. Glue the two strips together at right angles, as shown. Now fold one over the other to make a concertina.

4 Stick one end of the tail into the matchbox lid, as shown, using double-sided tape.

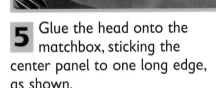

5 Glue the head onto the matchbox, sticking the center panel to one long edge, as shown.

6 Thread a needle with a double length of cotton, and make a knot at the end. Push the needle through the matchbox, as shown, to make a hanging loop. Push the tongue into the matchbox. Glue in place. To finish, stick gift-wrap ribbon to the dragon's tail.

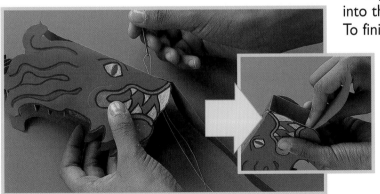

Ask an adult to help you use a sharp needle.

Dancing bear

This funny dancing bear is a traditional toy from Russia. The legs and arms are attached to a long length of thread. If you pull the thread, the bear will dance for you.

YOU WILL NEED

red cardboard	paper fasteners
tracing paper and pencil	crochet thread
scissors	large needle
colored pencils	cotton thread
felt-tip pens	

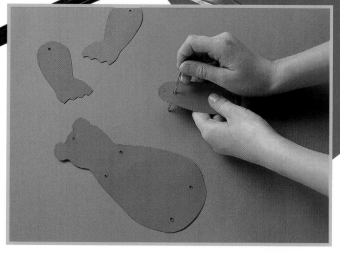

1 Trace the patterns for the bear on page 30. (See Making patterns, on page 5.) Cut the shapes out of red cardboard. Using a needle, make holes in the shapes, in the positions shown on the patterns. To make the large holes, push the needle through the shape several times. Ask an adult to help you do this.

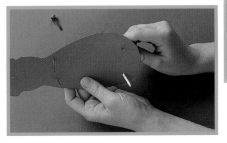

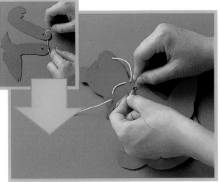

2 Draw the bear's features with a felt-tip pen. Decorate the body, arms, and legs with colored pencils.

3 Turn all the shapes over so they are facing down. Push paper fasteners through the large holes in the body, from front to back, as shown.

4 Thread crochet thread through the small holes in the top half of the legs and arms. Do not tie the ends together yet. Attach the arms and legs to the body by pushing them onto the paper fasteners. Bend over the ends on the fasteners to hold the arms and legs in place.

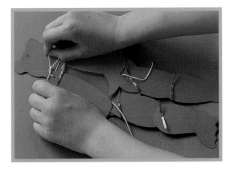

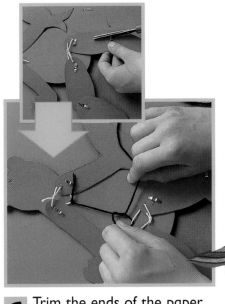

5 Attach the bottom half of the legs to the top half with paper fasteners. Put the arms and legs in line with the body. Now tie the ends of the thread holding the arms together and tie the thread holding the legs together.

6 Trim the ends of the paper fasteners with scissors, as shown. Ask an adult to help you. To finish, tie a long length of thread to the loop holding the arms together. Now tie the thread to the loop holding the legs. To make the bear dance, just pull the thread.

Ask an adult to help you use a needle and the paper fasteners.

Treasure box

This pretty box is based on a design for an old English tea caddy (a box for holding tea leaves). It's decorated with paper quills, gold paint, and glass nuggets.

YOU WILL NEED

- small, empty cardboard carton with sloping lid
- gold spray paint
- quilling pen (from a craft shop)
- thin cardboard
- glass nuggets (from a craft shop)
- beads
- stickers
- scissors
- clear glue

1 Spray the carton gold on the outside. Ask an adult to help you do this. Let it dry. Now cut around the carton on three sides, as shown, about 1in (2.5cm) below the sloping top.

26

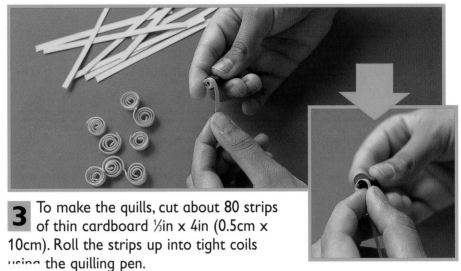

2 Spray the inside of the box gold. Ask an adult to help you do this. Cut the top of the box into points.

3 To make the quills, cut about 80 strips of thin cardboard ⅓in x 4in (0.5cm x 10cm). Roll the strips up into tight coils using the quilling pen.

4 Glue the quills all over the carton, leaving spaces for the glass nuggets, stickers, and beads. Spray gold paint all over the carton. Ask an adult to help

Ask an adult to help you use the spray paint. Use the paint outdoors if you can.

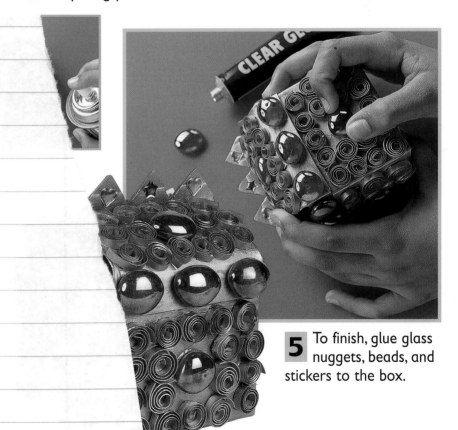

5 To finish, glue glass nuggets, beads, and stickers to the box.

Japanese fan

Fans were first made in Japan hundreds of years ago. Make the one shown here, with its pretty leaf and flower pattern, to keep you cool on a hot day or to use as a decoration.

YOU WILL NEED

red cardboard	pencil
black cardboard	white paper (for stencil)
black poster paint	clear glue
sponge	black felt-tip pen
scissors	red thread, 2yd (2m)
tracing paper	

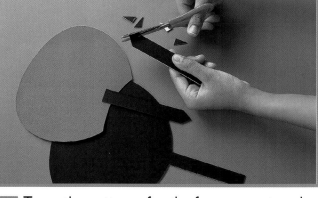

1 Trace the patterns for the fan, crescent, and handle on page 31. (See instructions on page 5.) For the fan, lay the half pattern face down on black cardboard. Rub over the outline with a pencil. The shape will appear on the cardboard. Flip the tracing over, line up the pattern, and trace back over the pencil lines to complete the whole fan. Cut out the shape. Cut a crescent from red cardboard in the same way. Cut three handles from black cardboard. Glue one handle to the bottom of the crescent, as shown.

2 Trace the flower and leaf patterns on page 31, and make a stencil out of white paper. (See Making stencils, on page 5.) Hold the stencil in place on the crescent, and sponge black paint onto the - crescent through the cut-out shapes.

3 When the paint is dry, carefully glue the crescent onto the fan, as shown.

4 Glue the extra handles to the main fan handle to strengthen it. Touch up the edges with a black felt-tip pen.

5 To make a tassel, wind red thread around your fingers to make a loop. Tie a short piece of thread around the top of the loop. Cut through the loop at the bottom of the tassel. Tie the tassel to the handle of the fan.

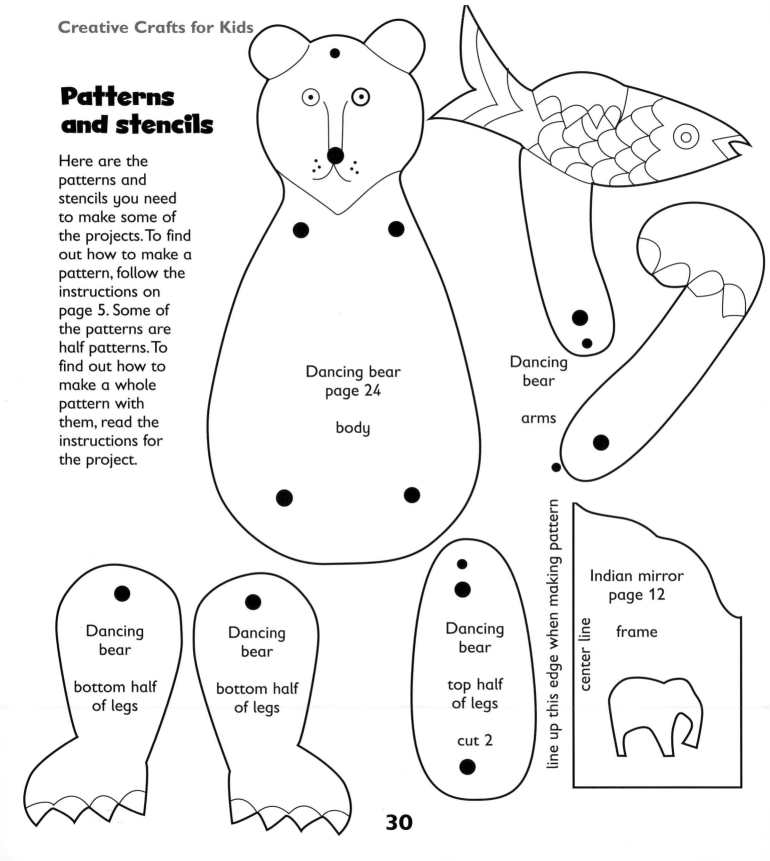

Creative Crafts for Kids

Patterns and stencils

Here are the patterns and stencils you need to make some of the projects. To find out how to make a pattern, follow the instructions on page 5. Some of the patterns are half patterns. To find out how to make a whole pattern with them, read the instructions for the project.

Dancing bear
page 24

body

Dancing bear

arms

Dancing bear

bottom half
of legs

Dancing bear

bottom half
of legs

Dancing bear

top half
of legs

cut 2

line up this edge when making pattern

center line

Indian mirror
page 12

frame

30

Japanese fan
page 28

For the Chinese dragon, the center panel must be the same width as the striking side of the matchbox.

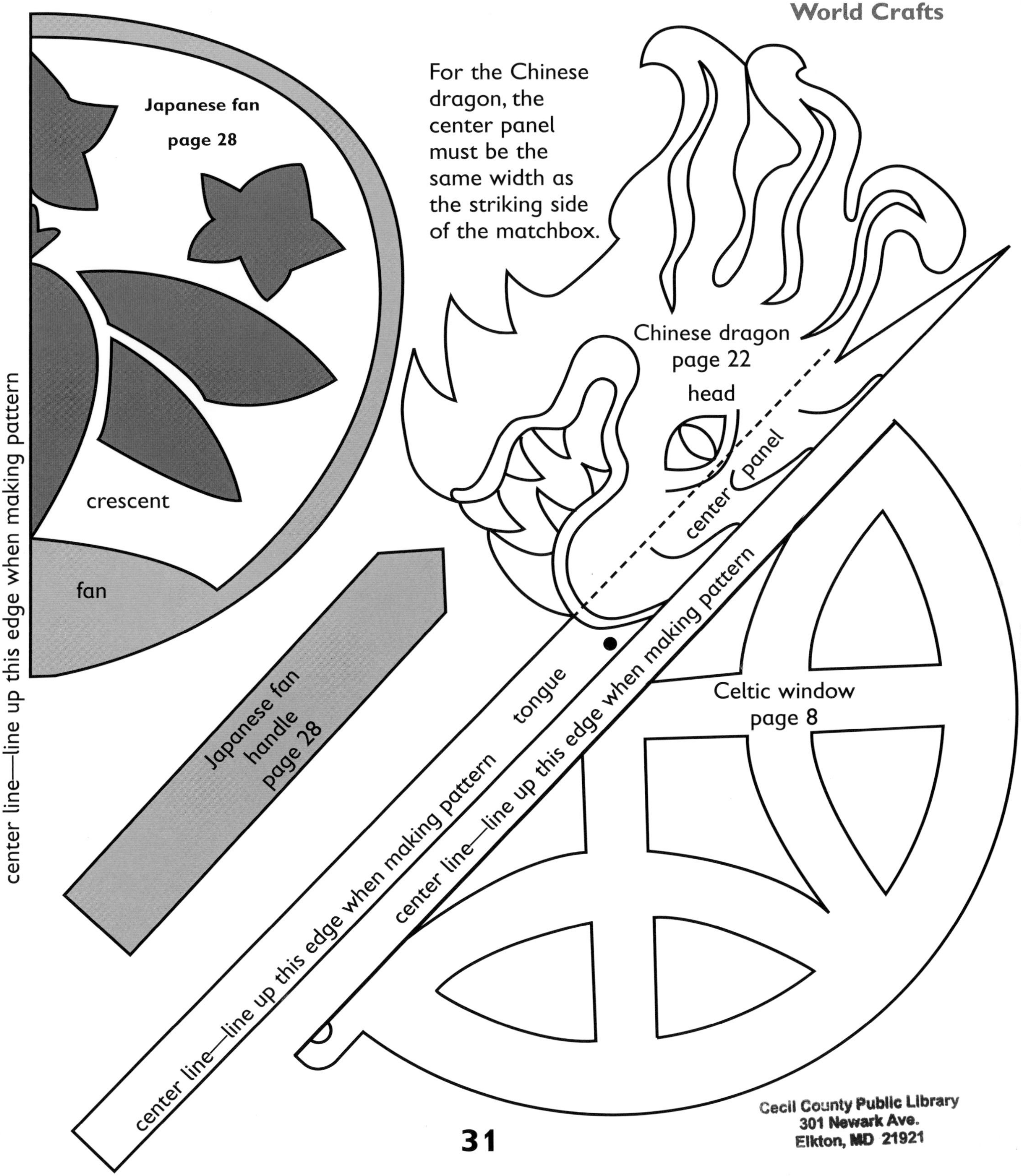

crescent

fan

Chinese dragon
page 22

head

center panel

center line—line up this edge when making pattern

Japanese fan handle
page 28

tongue

center line—line up this edge when making pattern

center line—line up this edge when making pattern

Celtic window
page 8

31

Glossary

armadillo a mammal with a hard-plated body found in temperate and tropical regions of the Americas

burrow a hole an animal digs in the ground for shelter

cellophane a thin, transparent, waterproof material used for wrapping and covering

ceremonial having to do with a ceremony, or series of actions done for special occasions

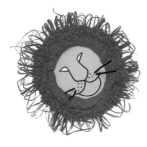

concertina a small octagonal accordion with button keys

Mardi Gras a name for the day before the beginning of the Christian time of Lent

PVA glue one of the most common glues. "PVA" stands for polyvinyl acetate.

raffia fiber in the form of flexible straw-colored ribbons used in making mats, baskets, and other products

stencil to apply a design to a surface using a pattern

tambourine a shallow drum with jingling metal disks in its frame, held in one hand and played by shaking it or striking it with the other hand

tassel a bunch of loose threads tied together at one end that is used as decoration

varnish a substance that gives an object a protective gloss, or the act of applying this substance

Velcro a material of two strips, one consisting of hooks and the other consisting of loops, that fasten together

Index